I0764361

Arriving on Time

ARRIVING ON TIME

Poems by

Wil Mills

Edited by

Kathryn Oliver Mills

Measure Press
Evansville, Indiana

Printed in the United States of America
First Edition

The text of this book is composed in Baskerville.
Edited by Kathryn Oliver Mills
Composition by R.G.
Manufacturing by Ingram.

Mills, Wil, 1969–2011
Arriving on Time / by Wil Mills — 1st ed.

ISBN-13: 978-1-939574-21-3
ISBN-10: 1-939574-21-8
Library of Congress Control Number: 2017910181

Measure Press
526 S. Lincoln Park Dr.
Evansville, IN 47714
http://www.measurepress.com/measure/

Acknowledgments

Wil was trying to publish this manuscript before he died, so his family is particularly grateful to Measure Press and Rob Griffith for publishing it. I have kept its general outline as well as its original dedication. However, realizing that they might not otherwise be published in book form, I have added several poems to this final version, and as a consequence have made a few changes to the earlier manuscript's order. I want to express my gratitude to Tim Steele, Alan Shapiro, and Raymond Oliver for commenting on this manuscript as I was editing it. Many thanks also to the poets who generously wrote blurbs for this book, and to Phoebe-Agnès for illustrating her father's work.

— Kathryn Oliver Mills

The author wishes to thank the editors of the publications in which these poems have appeared, sometimes in slightly different form.

The Hudson Review: "Stanzas for Kathryn"
Literary Imagination: "After the Fact"
Louisiana Literature: "Time in New Orleans," "The Funeral," "*Recordari*-Song," "Déjà-vu in Ocean Springs, Mississippi," and "Love Time, My Daughter"
The New Criterion: "Black Skimmers on the Gulf Coast" and "Remembering Grand Isle"
The New Republic: "Rest Stop, Alabama"
The Oxford American: "Thanksgiving on the Gulf"
Poetry: "At Dauphin Island" and "An Equation for my Children"
The Sewanee Review: "The Flower Beds of War"
Sewanee Theological Review: "Jack Daniel in the Lion's Den"
Shenandoah: "Sailing to Horn Island" and "Walter Anderson on the Chandelleurs"
The Southern Review: "The Genius of Hardin County"
Swallow: "Fondue Analysis"
Tar River Poetry, "Making the Cradle"
The Yale Review: "A Letter to Myself as a Young Man"

For Kathryn, Benjamin, and Phoebe-Agnès

CONTENTS

I. Louisiana Souvenir

II. Tennessee Home

III. Gulf Coast Highway

IV. The Heart's Arithmetic

I. Louisiana Souvenir

My Grandfather in the London Blitz

A Sunday morning. He was twenty-nine,
In church, and unaware that right next door,
A German rocket in a steep decline
Would change *my* life when he was ninety-four.

Can history anticipate itself?
That rocket spared his life, but, in my head,
The self of time flew forward in my flesh
And detonated out of how he said
The blast had so completely burned the air
That flocks of starlings in a tree outside
Had fallen, stunned, not dead.
                                        What changed me there
Was hearing his story, his voice, our being alive,
Our being part of the significance
That all those starlings lifted up at once.

Time Capsule

A wax recording of the sing-along
A hundred years ago. Thanksgiving Day.
Between the talk, the static, and the song,
We hear the silverware and someone say
That snow had just begun to fall. And then
The whistle-hiccup of a cuckoo clock
Above the spinet tells us *when* and *when,*
That time is soft of hearing; like a rock,
It listens in the ground, remembering
With fossils that cannot forget the fish.
We hear the singing, thankful it can bring
The living voices of the dead to wish
Us well when our Novembers fail to please
With snow that falls on ground that doesn't freeze.

After the Fact

Lightning spiraled down an oak;
Its fire both tapped the wind
And wrapped a die of threaded smoke
Around the bark it skinned.
And in the ashes of the grass,
It left our quarter horses
Smoking, bloated with foul gas,
Buzzards on their corpses.
Their manes and hooves had blasted free
Around the blood that pooled.
Their eyes had boiled instantly
Then just as quickly cooled.

It happened while I lay in bed;
I went there after the fact
To see for myself, to wrap my head
Around the proof I lacked.
But at the scene I shut my eyes,
And when I did, I swear
That something let me visualize
A world that wasn't there,
The way those horses might have seen
Before the fire fell —
No longer color blind between
The poles of heaven and hell —
The colors of stars, all night *and* day,
Well-digger's only view,
Or chimneysweeper's dream, astray,
Released, in the chimney flue.

Louisiana whistled in me
A song of rotted pine,
Of logs that fell a century
Ago and left no sign.
But Daddy said that, as a boy,
He walked the woods at night
And saw what dirt did not destroy:
A poltergeist of light
Where phosphorous in rotted wood
Still burned a shape of trees.
So I remembered it for good,
As if his memories
Were mine, his story the proof I prize,
Though after the fact, in trust,
What I believe without my eyes,
Believing because I must.

Mamma's Loom

I remember Mamma winding yards of thread
Around my sisters' arms. I watched her hands
Turn over and over themselves in somersaults
To fill what seemed like webs of half-made cloth
Inside her loom. It opened when she pressed the pedals,
And closed when the shuttle slid from end to end.

I often sat beside the dangling ends
And ran my fingers over the tightened threads
As if to strum a silent harp whose pedals
Almost kept a foot-tap rhythm with my hands.
I watched her while she rolled her cloth,
Her hands out front, rubbing sweat and salt
In the shuttle wood. Then, doing somersaults
Around her loom, I played with the tangled ends,
And poked my face in the raveled gauze of cloth.
I remember the cardiac clatter through the thread.
Then going to sleep, and waking up, her hands
Still throwing the shuttle, her feet still on the pedals.

All that was years ago, when I heard pedals,
When I learned my trick of somersaults.
Today she rarely ever weaves. Her hands
Don't need to tend her loom's unraveled ends.
But when she sees me now, she cuts loose thread
From shirts I wear, reminding me of cloth
She used to weave as if she thought to clothe
Her children with a fabric soft as flower petals,

Or with cotton paper made of shredded thread,
A place to paint the shades of burning salt
She primed in us, the colors in a vein, what bends
All through a body, flowing to the hands.

I look at my palms and see instead *her* hands,
As if to read the subtle pattern of her cloth
Still printed there, still fitting well, though age distends
The memory of harnesses and pedals.
Today they're suffering the slow assault
Of dust and disuse. The shuttle is empty of thread.

I put my feet to the pedals, my hands on the frame
And I can almost smell the salt in the cloth,
And feel the ends of thread on my face.

Daddy's Bed

He used to sleep here, tuckered, with dirty feet
When, as a boy, he'd climbed all day in trees,
Then climbed in bed, as if in a fort, hands down
More solid than his tree house or the tree house
In his dreams.
                                And then he grew. The footboard
Curled his body, made it fit the mattress,
Bending him, a question mark on the mattress,
Germ of a thought with hands and feet.
It's still unfolding in him, and in me.
                                                                His footboard-
Fences hold the roots and dreams of family trees
That someday I'll inherit — with the bed of tree-house-
Dreams, its living hardwood — hand-me-down.
I'll take it, and whatever they should hand me, down
The ladder, onto the same old mattress
Where my body curls today. Am I a guest in the house?
I have returned, and always will. What I attempted to defeat
By leaving it, is still a familiar shade of trees,
Still my lumber, log, root, trunk, board foot.

But this time, home for a funeral, Daddy's footboard
Holds my ankles back. This hand-me-down
Of dreams and days he played in trees,
It still impedes me when I roll.
                                                        I hear the mattress
Overflow with memories of moving feet.
Visitor-son. Where is my house?

This was *his* barefoot dream, *his* treehouse.
When *he* climbed out of bed, each foot bored
Down and held like roots instead of feet.
And this is where he planted me, by handing down
An answer to the question on his mattress:
How to find the living wood of family trees.

What dreams do not uncurl from family trees?
A haunting in the genes? Oh no, my acorn couldn't house
My dream. Its message printed briefly on his mattress,
No raised bed, no garden plot of six-foot boards.
I took the question *and* the answer handed down
Together, and I left. I was the sound of running feet,
And now the toes that touch the footboard.
I hold my ear to the mattress, hearing wind
In the treehouse like a dream come hand-me-down.

The Funeral

St. Francisville, Louisiana

Under akimbo live oak limbs and loads
Of Spanish moss and resurrection fern,
It's clear that merely being here forebodes
A kind of irony that I'll discern
If I can find the words objectively;
Despite these wreaths of dying "baby's breath,"
You were the doctor who delivered me.
You saw my In, I see you Out in death.

Old man, mid-husband, shaman, you were the seer
Peering through the ocean of a girl
Where I'd begun to listen, shaped like an ear,
Uncoiling my little bones in mother-of-pearl.
What did you hear? my fins becoming hands?
My heart valves ticking, delicate and fast,
And sounding like a million grains of sand
Inside the silhouette of an hour glass?
I heard a story of the Spanish Main,
A tiny pirate with a single wish
To cast and also be the silver seine
That caught the fisher and the herring fish.
Starlight was still a dream I couldn't see,
But I could hear it weave a mesh of lines
Between the stars to make a net for me,
A chart of constellations and designs.
It told the story I was meant to live
By warping from the end to my beginning,
So the stars became like holes in a sieve

Around my little atoms and their spinning.
But in the artificial light and time,
I felt a trace of the pain an old man feels.
You held me by the ankle bones to prime
The fatal tendons of my infant heels,
And, screaming my exuberant despair,
The only way I knew to prophesy,
I felt a chill, esthesias of air,
Once I was born, once I'd begun to die.

The second time we met in the world of dirt
When I was still invincible as hell
And you were old and drooling on your shirt,
I struggled then, as now, with how to spell
The moment into meaning, my words unsure.
And, even though your mind had gone to seed,
Gone back to the womb, I told you, "Thank you, sir."
You answered, "All my goods are guaranteed,"
A tragic-comic flash of clarity.
O, jester, doorman, doctor all in one!
O, my deliverer, my enemy!
Is death the guarantee that I have won?
We're all invincible until we die,
Struck down by a minor blow, a prick, a sting,
Learning that our bravado was a lie,
As did Achilles and the Fisher King.

And in this *liebestod* that we rehearse
At weddings, Christenings, and funerals,
We look for words (a joke, a prayer, a curse),
Something to organize the intervals
And ironies of life. Or we simply say,

"Hello," "farewell," and mean it like a vow
To keep by merely living the passion play
Of birth and closure in the here and now.

Tristesse in April

This is the week I've played Chopin,
The *Etude number three*, the one
My parents played repeatedly
The April when I almost died.
I lay inventing memories
I'd never have: rice paper dreams,
Paper made from popcorn or egg whites.

Houses are made of wood and time,
And, though the house where I was sick is gone,
I can shut my eyes and walk all through it.
That boy I used to be is dead,
But my body still remembers him
In flashes: an impulse to run, climb trees.
Sometimes I check my watch and think
The second hand has stopped; it lags
Above the five, not ending time
But making it more infinite,
An eternity outside of time
Before the hand continues ticking.
Is that where forgotten memories go
To be refined, made better than life?
Is life a practice run, a study,
Of what we think that place is like?

Between the *Etude's* movements, the work
Of theme, variation, and return,
We practice missing the intervals.

The middle section is the hardest:
Diminished chords and accidentals!
Tristesse is in the line between
How *this* and *that* can almost touch,
Making us want to stop the flow
To feel the gaps, to count the rings
Of trees we first cut down, learning
That nostalgia prophesies the past
Where every nick of time is a bird
We kill, as Audubon did, drawing
Its beauty, wiring it into poses,
Trying to paint it as it rotted.

The last of the dogwood flowers flutter
Upwards in a gust, like paper,
Like boyhood, back as a moment's ghost
To land on my grill and vaporize.

Time in New Orleans

Once again in the city of rain,
I've come eavesdropping down the streets
Where even the corner signs invite
A passer-by to listen in:
Prytania, Bourbon, Poydras, Canal.
They tell of gravel and bits of sand
That pigeons left in cornices
To gargle down the copper gutters
And wash their sibilance on brick.

On Jackson Square, I also hear
The soothing voices think aloud
About the merry-go-round of signs;
It never changes year to year.
They've almost got it down to a science,
Dismal science, hope for hire
In Pidgin English that provides
A kind of solace for *demain.*
They tilt the running coffee grounds
And read the cards and dirty palms
Of anxious customers who think
That chance is never hazardous
And that the pre-determined future
Somehow leaves them wiggle room.

In Pirate's Alley, though, I hear
The talking of a thought that feels
Like memory turned inside-out,

Or like random thoughts from years before,
What I forgot because, back then,
I didn't know how it foretold
My being here today.
Or is it
What everyone is feeling here,
Yearning for something lost in time?
New Orleans lets me walk along
As if inside a mind that holds
Then offers up its memories
Freely to those who pay attention.
It lets me own these streets and own
The way they're haunted by themselves
In some collective déjà-vu.

There are no seasons here, just fronts
That cycle in, and most are wet,
And this is a city made for rain,
The kind that falls so late at night
That people seldom notice how
A filthy sidewalk cleans itself,
How signs and traffic lights demur
To the color of shutters, blending dark
And demulcent tones, *cafe-au-lait*,
Mulatto-light.
New Orleans knows
Why languages have words that mingle
Sentiment with time and place:
Nostalgia, *Sehnsucht, Hiraeth, Saudade,*
Words for inconsolable
Desire and longing, words that mean
What only being here can help

Me almost comprehend, spelling
How preterits are prescient
Of the future's imperfection,
Where time is a given,
Like a present.

A Letter to Myself as a Young Man

I.
Here in the room that still belongs to you,
A room that now does not belong to me,
The years between us curve as if upon
A hanging silver chain.
                                        My being here
Has drawn together where the ends are held,
Making a catenary smile, and then
A single line of yesterday and now
Where time runs vertically, then not at all.

For once, I see you clearly, eye to eye.
You're sweating in your bed, the windows open,
And the cricket chorus hasn't quite replaced
The noise of combine engines in your ears.
That's how it is for you, night after night
Beneath a ceiling fan that tries and fails
To give you some oblivion against
Your being seventeen years old or so.

I'm writing now because you're deep in thought:
It seems to you that time has almost stopped
And made a quiet place behind your eyes.
In fact, my writing you *is* what you feel.
I am the memory you will become,
The déjà-vu that catches in your throat

And makes you think that everything in life
Has happened like a script, already known,
Already told in countries of the past.

I'm writing now because you're listening,
Entirely present, empty of desire
That gnaws you. It's an animal, I know,
The fiercest kind of hunger, ravenous
As only teenage men can understand.
You feel the sluggish cadences of life,
And try to race ahead, impatiently,
To find the future and its holiday.
But then it keeps elapsing into past,
Behind your back. No matter how you strain
Against the flow, its motion sets a pace
And carries life along, as if to tell
A story from the rhythm it had made
Without a single synonym for Time.

II.
Tomorrow when you look at clouds too much
You'll lose your swath. The cutter bar will dive
And hit the biggest ant hill in the field,
Clogging the teeth and blade with dirt and grass.
You'll shut the engine down beside a pond,
Walk over to the edge, lie down, and let
The back of your head and ears sink under water.

Your frame will slowly lose the shimmy-shake
Of universal joints and the PTO.
Beneath the silent brightness of the sky,

There won't be any noise, for once, and clouds
That pile above the trees will seem to halt,
As if in step with you. While anchored there,
You'll feel the planet turning slowly past.
Remember me tomorrow when the clouds
Traverse your eye in sync with how you breathe,
The up and down. I'm here to tell you, boy,
As soon as you can feel the pace, you'll learn
That "happen" is the finest word around,
By chance, a risk, a hazard of the dice,
And yet it couldn't be more definite.
The dice are loaded, as they always are.
The angel always says, "Fear not! Abide!"
The story comes to pass, (not running late
Or early) arriving when it should, on time.

Remembering Grand Isle

They brought me here before my memory.
And yet each time I see where I once came,
My recollection is peremptory.
Past perfect and the present are the same.

I see, and I have seen, the myrtles lean
With live oaks in the vector of the rains.
They're written here, both stiff and evergreen,
Engraved invisibly by hurricanes.

One cannot see the stylus of the storm
Except for how it chisels limb and leaf.
The infant's eyes record no shape or form,
And yet our hearts are carved like bas-relief.

When place and buried memories combine
With my todays and yesterdays of line,
The folds and wrinkles of the past appear.
The mind itself becomes a souvenir.

II. Tennessee Home

My Wedding Toast

I.
To you, my wife of only several hours,
While our new kith and kin enjoy their last
Few bites of our first conjugal repast,
I propose again, a toast for what is ours
Today and ever in the future.
                                        I lift
My glass to you. This life we now begin
Will always name today its origin,
And looking back to it will be a gift.

II.
As in the etymology of "toast,"
When bread was dunked in wine to flavor praise
For someone by a lover, friend, or host,
Dear family, we don't need bread to raise;
Just whisper Kathryn's name above your wine,
And it will taste as sweet as what is mine.

My Sleeping She

To begin with. Morning moves
In another part of the house.
I am at work. How clumsily
My listening picks up the calm
Of something restful, other breath.
My wife is sleeping late today.
Her other breath climbs out of sigh
And stillness, rooms removed from me,
Though near enough. My sleeping she.
This her of me beside myself.
And listening I hear the ease-
Air blown, escaping after words,
Silent phrases, like the hushed
Shape of spoil behind a bird.
And I am waiting for a sense
To show itself, pausing straight
In my chair, in our tight house that seems
To lift and sink along with her.
A sussurance of curtain flesh.
Awake, I hear the growing sense.
It whispers something in the walls,
"Your wife is sleeping late and you
Have chosen this. And you will choose
It always. Blanket halcyon.
Her other breath. A life to end with."

Changes in the Summer Garden

The trillium are dead,
Dissolved along with daffodils,
And since late May, the phlox
Have gone to seed and fallen
Where the violets grow thick.

My garden gloves still reek of green,
A smell of unwashed clothing, sweat
Allowed to dry in cotton shirts.
The piles of weeds above the hill
Turn brown before their time.

But this is not unpleasant anymore,
I've learned to love the smell of open earth,
The taste of water from cupped hands.
Small bulbs spread out below the vinca.
Periwinkle takes the wall before my eyes.

When post oak leaves are full of light
I wash my hands and stop to watch
The lightning bugs appear at dusk
To sprinkle their brief emeralds
Above my darkened flower beds.

Cicadas rise and fall in swells
Of rhythmic synchronicity,
But fireflies make no sound at all,

A syncopated silence, strewn
Delightfully around my porch.

Lately in the morning when I smell
Swing pillows left outside at night
I like to walk between the beds
And yank out weeds I missed before
Where morning glories choke the ferns.

The summer should remain this way,
Each wave of new perennials
Uncurling from the dirt, their blooms
Replacing past varieties
That have faded and gone to seed.

Who can say why all the beds
Of hasta lift their stalks of indigo,
Each one together on the chosen day.
I've watched them dripping after rain
Late in the day, almost new myself.

It changes every hour now,
By growing over borders like
The tendency of rising streams.
And I go back to weeding, work
That never ends beginning.

Fondue Analysis

For Kathryn

The way I analyze a sign or symbol
Is not romantic like a sonnet for you,
Unless I show you how things re-assemble.

As with gruyere and bread in hot fondue
Whose combination only needs a flame
For the prosy recipe to melt our hearts,
The art is in the mixture, not the parts.

You burn the cheese. I drop the bread. We blame
Each other at the pot.
                                        My Dear, we sense
How poetry can smolder into prose
When life and art resist a confluence.
But love attaches passages then grows
To conjugate the parts. Our lives combine
With art, converse in prose, and fall in line.

An Explanation Owed to my Child in the Womb

For Benjamin, conceived on my birthday

Dear birthday child,
before you started moving,
When you were shaped like a tiny question mark,
We noticed how our anniversaries
Had overlapped, a thing astrologers
Might try to prove was no coincidence
With star maps, almanacs, and calendars.
But even with their knowledge of the sky
They couldn't solve the mystery of you
Or how miraculous it felt the instant
That you began to twinkle in my eye.

I'm no astrologer and don't condone
The way they see without relationship,
But wise men still look up at stars and wonder.
It's still the oldest curiosity,
No different from the Star of Bethlehem.
Each shining body has significance.
One life affects the way another moves.
And time is ripening. You're due in June,
Though here in the land of clocks, I wonder what,
If anything, could matter to you now
When all you know is light and sound reduced
To rhythm, lung and atrium in sync.
Your world is made of timing more than time.

For several years, I've had a mental quest
To understand how time and light are kin.
A beam of light is made of particles
As well as waves that oscillate through space.
The speed of this determines how we feel
When years are broken down in increments.
But all I think about is water, say,
When there's a dewdrop caught below a twig.
A morning breeze will make it move in light,
Unleashing red and green and blue and gold.
It has a musical effect on me
As if each color played a certain note,
A xylophone of shine in water's prism.

It's true that light is made of color bands,
And Van Gogh believed each color had a sound,
And Satie thought every note suggested color.
Those men were geniuses, though, in the end,
They weren't entirely sane, so there's a risk
For me to think that light is audible.
But lately I've been hearing nursery rhymes
That jingle through the trees all afternoon;
It sounds like what the shepherds might have heard
In Bethlehem.
Once, on a winter's day
When it was bright, not a cloud in the sky,
And blocks of window light were on the floor,
I held your mother in the shine and let
The muntin shadow-lines conform around
Her belly's ever-growing curvature.
I wondered how much you could hear in there
And couldn't help but think of Keats and how

The figures on a Grecian urn had caused
His reverie of music locked in time.
Are you a little reveler who moves
To unheard melodies and rhythms of red?
Do you hear chimes of light slowed down to a glisten?
No doubt the sun was bright enough for you
To notice how the light turned purest crimson;
You lurched inside her as my fingers traced
The sash's shadow pattern over you.

Light changes everything it penetrates.
And, in the press and harvest of a marriage,
Human waters join as living wine,
What Jesus showed the wedding guests at Cana
Then made his blood live on in memory
By sips of wine, clear light turned into claret.

It's likely that you'll grow to disagree
With my unscientific thoughts on time,
But someday you'll feel sunlight on your face
And have a child yourself and think you hear
A ringing sound from stars or drops of water,
Proving the issue: that we're next of kin.

This Work is a Church

For W.B.

After the sawmill engine's killed
And silences return,
I stack my girder beams and sills
And feel my muscles burn.

Hard labor leaves a pleasant ache
In arm and back and wrist
And loosens me as if to make
My task a hypnotist.

If "idle hands are the devil's shop"
Where fingers stay at rest,
Then finding rhythm on the job
Of carpentry is blessed.

The world of cubicle and screen
Disdains this repetition.
But in monotony I've seen
A chore unveil a vision.

This work is a church that bodies build,
A structure made of movement.
Its chantey frames a room that's filled
With intervals of music.

Oh, let me live in the vacant spaces
Where that music floats.
I'll dance in the silent time that graces
Air between the notes.

And drifting deeper into prayer
With muscles sore and stinging,
I'll let my work build a winding stair
In chapels of my singing.

Stacking Lumber

for R.O.

I.
This morning by degrees,
Like even the oaks in icing,
I believe in the dance of trees.
They implore me, enticing
With stillness I understand.
They shift but hold their ground,
Spilling and filling sand
That sifts before it's sound.

I cultivate a rhythm:
Balance-to-counterbalance.
They result in algorithms
With poise and equipoise.
My arms are metronomes
Like pendulums upside down,
To chart the math of poems.
I bend to be profound.

Chore becomes a chantey
By dissolving noise in spells
To restore my inner shanty.
They solve the math of bells
That sway a single line.
Like hour glass chalices,
My play is the keeping of time
Towers chime in my palaces.

II.
I turn, pick up a board, and swivel back.
The wood's own weight helps me complete my swing,
Lean slightly out, and let the lumber drop.

My tablets pile, collecting deeper thunks,
A sunken knocking that oars and gunwales make,
The human sound a whale might hear and fear.
Time dissolves around me and my hands,
Slowing by racing backwards into calm
The way it may have been when, as a boy,
Einstein already dreamed that he could ride
A beam of light to see if that would render
Clocks irrelevant.
                                        I ride that beam;
I turn, pick up a board, and swivel back
In the music of motion, a lovely dissonance
I hear as choruses of humpback whales
That haunt the nautilus inside my ear.

III.
This morning by degrees, I cultivate a rhythm: chore becomes a chantey
Like even the oaks in icing, balance-to-counterbalance. By dissolving noise in spells
I believe in the dance of trees. They result in algorithms to restore my inner shanty.
They implore me, enticing with poise and equipoise. They solve the math of bells
With stillness I understand. My arms are metronomes that sway a single line.
They shift but hold their ground, like pendulums upside down, like hour glass chalic
Spilling and filling sand to chart the math of poems. My play is the keeping of time
That sifts before it's sound. I bend to be profound. Towers chime in my palaces.

Tennessee Double-Wide

Endless hectares in the hills of oak,
By certain nooks of ferns and moss, invoke
A breath of yester-light, pristine, intact,
From "days of yore" before divided tracts
And parcels of a transit lens had miled
And mapped the wilderness no longer wild.

We've come to this in all of Tennessee,
Especially where the rocky tops and trees
Have grown accustomed to a lack of lines.
Defined but arbitrary here, the survey signs
And rights-of-way no longer follow terrain;
Where boulders ridge; how streams are cut by rain;
Expanse that used to be delineated by
The lichen's doily edge; a tree line; sky.

Today it's thirty, seven-acre-lots,
Each one a hundred paces wide, long slots
Of ingress-egress, where the denizens
Of here-and-now descend by the dozen and cleanse
A woodland site of understory brush.
Here are the sounds of chainsaw, backhoe, crusher-
Run of limestone gravel side to side,
A level surface for the double-wide.

The Jar Garden

"I placed a jar in Tennessee"
— Wallace Stevens

A snow that fell two days ago is still
In patches where the shadows keep their chill,
And water standing in the cups and jars
Has frozen solid near the passing cars
Where, on my sawmill, I make boards from pines
And oaks cut down below the power lines.

My breath is visible. My hands are stiff.
But the work is wonderful especially if
I notice how the season beautifies
The noise and trash around me; it almost cries
That winter is a feast of ice and light
Despite the poles and pulsing wires drawn tight
In ambient static and electric blare
To shock the silence of a clearing's air;
Despite the gouges over stone beneath
An outcrop scored with backhoe-bucket teeth;
Despite the windrows of debris to burn,
And everywhere, discarded near a fern
Or tree, the random trash that workmen threw:
Tobacco wrappers and the residue
Of sandwich foil, cans, and bottle-caps
That linger, rusting as the days elapse.

But one large jar that landed upside-down
Defies the ugliness that came from town.
It's almost lovely how the moss has grown

Inside its dome, as if someone could have thrown
It there that way on purpose, like an act
Of placing order that the woods had lacked,
Allowing what before would never grow:
A greenhouse-garden in the silent snow.
Smiling, I think of Stevens' poetry.
Here is the jar he placed in Tennessee!
It's still as round as when it showed that Man
Bewilders nature just because he can,
Because the slightest touch or *trace des mains*
Will garden savage land as our *jardin,*
Planted in rows, or painted into frames,
Or tamed in languages with nouns and names.

I stop, turn off my loud machinery,
And stand in something of a reverie.
In stillness now, between the cigarette butts
And trenches made from truck and tractor ruts,
Pretending that I don't exist, and then,
Wishing that I could breathe the oxygen
Inside that jar, I want to grow the rhyme
And reason of its nameless place and time
In every word and syllable I sing
To keep their meaning from meandering.

Treowe: An Etymology

The English language is a living thing
Which over time has had the sense to ring
Its rhyme and reason with the symmetry
Of roots and branches in a family tree.
That's no coincidence.
                                        The distant kin
Of certain pithy terms claim origin
From ancient trees that no one understood
Until the first codex had come from wood
And there were clerics who could read and teach
From books that got their letters from the beech.

But long before the folio and poem
Had been pressed together in a tome,
Before the logs were kept on tablets hewn
Of oak or elm, before the druid's rune,
There grew a seedling noun that ramified
The names of *Tree* and *Truth* and then it died.
Its sound was solid, finely grained and grooved,
As was its meaning: "That which cannot be moved."

Making the Cradle

All in winter while the lion's mane
Presided over sky too vast to measure,
I set out scraps of walnut lumber saved
From cabinet shops and studied how the grain
Had grown and then was cut. It gave me pleasure,
The kind when, looking at the stars, I've braved
The cold to see Orion keeping time
With Leo in a pattern like a rhyme.

It's said that aborigines can hear
The stars, and several times when I have seen
A meteor, there seemed to be a sound,
A muffled whistle through the atmosphere.
I've heard it planing knots in oak where scenes
Of grain in radiating lines abound.
Their patterns look like solar systems drawn
In books, elliptical by how they're sawn.

This is the joy in a cradle-maker's heart:
To build a little bed and make it sound,
To learn the curvature of crescent moons,
Their delicate meniscus, all with art
So rudimentary it becomes profound.
The walnut whispers and the starlight croons.
I'll make this cradle by the sky and swing
Our child to what the constellations sing.

Naming our Daughter

For Phoebe-Agnès

Dear little distaff, on St. Agnes' Eve
We brought you home, a night when legends state
That maidens see in dream, if they believe,
The men they'll marry on some future date.
Someday you'll hope for love and feel that haste
To see the past or future, much less between.
But now you're much too small and far too chaste
For dreams of men and hope in things unseen.

That night we also saw the moon's eclipse
When you were perfectly oblivious
To orbits overlapping in ellipse.
To us, the shining sign was obvious,
Foreshadowing your name along with ice
That hung below your brother's rocking horse;
The snow that turned to hail and fell like rice
At weddings; footprints melting on the porch.
I memorized each little thing as though
They all were somehow relevant beyond
The goings-on when you were born. I know
That someday all of it will correspond
To how we heard the sound of French around
The name *Agnès* that still means "pure." Its sound
Combined with *Phoebe*, meaning "bright as the moon,"
Both attributes that suit you from the womb.
You shone like gold, so we couldn't second-guess
The name that rose in us: Phoebe-*Agnès*.

Stanzas for Kathryn

I.
I love how bodies move, the way they sway,
Especially indoors where limbs obey
An architect's equivalent of grammar;
It's found in well-made houses like a glamour
On anybody's stride if walls and doors
Allow a natural traverse of floors,
Much like the spell of spoken words that ring
Inside the stricture of their structuring.

Just as a well-turned phrase can make the sound
And meaning of its language more profound,
A stanza can arrange the mind to walk
In patterns like a dance; good walls can talk
Of sonnets built in pretty rooms, of grace
Like chamber suites composed inside the place.

II.
I've read the body language of our house
The way I think of taking off your blouse
And dress, then petticoat and lingerie,
To see the movement you've concealed all day.

Undressing walls until the frame shows through
Is not erotic unless I think of you
Since where I choose to place a door affects
The view I'll have, enhancing effects
On me when you step from the tub to dry.

Your motion has a power on my eye,
However inadvertent, and you should know
That, as with moves in some exotic show
Where dancers glide by choreography,
I have a plan for your geography.

III.

The world will tell us, trying to break our spell,
That marriage is a necessary hell.
And if we listened we might soon believe
And lose the movement that could help us cleave.
That's why in work to build our house I think
Of how we'll move together near the sink,
Or in the halls.
                                But in our circumstance
Without a house, it's odd to think of dance;
Our lives continue at a frantic pace
As if we thought to win the human race
By turning in circles in sickness and in health.

But it's a dance, in poverty or wealth,
That funnels our freedom if we learn the form
And love the steps that turn us through the storm.

IV.

It matters that you first saw the light of day
In San Francisco where the locals say
The air is sparkling like champagne, so clear
And filtered as it meets the bay.
                                                    But here

The light does not have that intensity.
I've brought you back to the hills of Tennessee,
So this small bungalow I'm building for you
Will have a lot of windows.
                                        There's no view
Of bays or bridges, only oaks and pines
To filter the wind. But when the summer shines
We'll have a quilt of light in every room.

Our son and child who's still inside your womb
Will grow in sight by how their parents see
The need to drink the day's transparency.

V.
You've heard me quip that, while you make the womb
Around our baby, I will make the room.
My play on words can try to hide how stressed
We are by both, but humor, at its best,
Is such a fluid thing it joins the joke
To what is true about the fun I poke.

In words, I think about the miracle
Your body works, how it's empirical
The way, by trial and struggle, we gain entry
To the greatest joy.
                                        But while my carpentry
Externalizes your internal task,
My puns mix Thing and Thought and make me ask
If life is *jeux de mots*, push come to shove.
Shaping words and things is a labor of love.

VI.
Rearing children is no *haute culture*.
It's more like husbandry or agriculture
With all the fencing and the fertilizer.

We aren't just fertile; now we're downright wiser
In all the chores. We've grown so *laissez-faire*,
At least in terms of dirt or germs they share.

But, as in farming, there is a higher art
To tending anything. All jobs impart
Their lessons over time by drawing on
The rudiments of life.
                                        It's dawning on
Me while I raise the children's walls how much
A parent needs a farmer's careful touch.

The art is seeing nature *as* an order.
Like farmer-artists, we give it shape and border.

VII.
The actuarial evidence has shown
That men who try to make it on their own
Die sooner than their married counterparts.

That doesn't mean they should "protect their hearts"
By finding trophy brides who're blonde, good looking,
Keep a spotless house, and do the cooking.

But I could be accused of such convenience,
Married to you, though it was grace, prevenience,
That led me to you providentially.

And I will say unconfidentially
This kitchen is a gift that says you're more
Than some man's "jackpot wife" or "perfect score."

I *will* live long by your chopping block and knife,
But that's not why I married you for life.

VIII.
A luthier can build a violin
By shaving top and back exactly thin
Enough to know the timbre it will make.
In carpentry, the margin of mistake
Is more forgiving, less a mystery,
But framing is a kind of luthery
The way I think of it.
                                        While planing the wood
Above our dining room I understood
By standing under it, how older cellos
Resonate a certain tone that mellows
Like a human voice.
                                        I said, "Amen,"
And heard the consonance of *M* and *N*
Where someday prayer will sound a compliment
To food like music in an instrument.

IX.
So much attention goes to special touches
Like mantles, chandeliers, and china hutches
That one might think our house will be defined
Exclusively by things we call refined.

It isn't likely that we'll spend our days
Entirely in the dining room with trays
Of silver, serving food to honored guests.

I hope our lives will have a certain zest,
But while I'm hanging pantry doors and trim
And caulking tiles around the bathtub rim,
I know that life will also be sublime
Where things become pedestrian with time.
I'll relish every nook and closet shelf
Where, next to you, I'll feel beside myself.

X.

The final touch will be your dressing room
Where, in a funny way, I'm more your groom
Than when I married you since I will build
Your closet, which I know will soon be filled
With all the clothes you own and hope to own.

It will also hold the wedding dress you'd sewn
To wear just once for me before it fell.
Its purpose was to cast a lasting spell
And not be worn again, a sentimental
Notion, but it's hardly incidental
That it worked.
                    I'm building your boudoir,
Housing romance like an old armoire,
And giving thought to you with each detail
Because I'm still the one who lifts your veil.

Blessing the House

For J.N.

When our house was finished, the noise and tools
Gave way to silence, to the dining room and rugs.
The place where I had made infernal noise
Became a sacramental space to eat,
And I could feel the fragile balance that
Divides a building site from living space.
Thieves break and enter. Fires rage. Trees fall.
I wanted a charm; I wanted words to curse
The rocks and scissors of the paper world.

It's purely superstitious, the oldest kind,
Needing a holy man to bless the structure
Or place a lucky spell upon the door,
But I asked my pastor and his wife for dinner
To say a prayer, ask God to bless our house.
(I didn't tell him how I wanted magic words
To leave a rainbow halo on the roof,
A secret shibboleth that we could utter.)

My wife prepared a *Carbonade Flamande*,
Beef chunks battered and stewed in Samuel Adams.
The children both behaved. But after dinner,
They squirmed and squabbled through the prayer.
That made me angry. I couldn't hear the words.
My son began to whine and kick his chair.
My daughter said she had to go to the potty!
Our pastor tried to finish up the prayer.

But then we heard my daughter yelling DOO DOO!
Brownish water flooded around her feet,
And, while I went downstairs to get a mop,
My pastor grabbed a towel, got on his knees,
And started mopping up the dirty water,
Plopping chunks back into the bowl as if
He did this everywhere he went for supper.
He grinned at me, happy as a child,

And didn't say a thing, but I could hear
His saying Nothing loud and clear, his posture,
The body language of a silent prayer.
I saw the young Teresa in India,
Her fingers slimed with someone's rotten skin.
I felt the sunshine of Assisi where
A single soul became a living prayer
That only birds and God could understand.

O, Lord, teach me to pray like Pastor Joe
Who blessed our house by how he moved inside it,
Signing a language with his dirty knees.
Let my body learn to speak it, too,
Moving through rooms I built, or anywhere,
A benediction from my bones
To bless the world.
Amen.

Gnossienne in Tennessee

When we say "to know," we mean "to recognize."
— Gadamer

Watching the rain in March,
Rain on the pear tree blossoms,
You can't say what it means,
But it's significant;
You know it when you see it,
An intuition running
Back to the Thing as if
The fallen petals washing
Whitely along the road
Perceive you, too, your NOW
That's won or lost across
How well you see what matters,
Things made phenomenal,
Their presence, as if the best
Epistemology
Is not explained (not "answer"
Or "question) but content
To stay on the tip of your tongue
And in the back of your mind,
A joy to recognize
By simply being there,
Your hourglass half full,
An understanding, gotten
And forgotten both at once.

III. Gulf Coast Highway

Rest Stop, Alabama

Even here the rows of urinals
Are "automatic-sensor-operated."
There's a laser eye that watches me
Unzip my pants so when I zip them up
It does the flushing for me seven times.

Above my head the ceiling has a speaker
Dishing out the sticky sentiments
Of country music, giving me advice,
Clichés and platitudes that tell how not
To live my life.
                                        Out in the lobby again,
A road map on the wall says, "You Are Here!"
And I can press a button near the map
To catch the weather service bulletin:
"It's partly cloudy in Mobile tonight."

I wonder why it matters if the clouds
Are out at night, and I remember how
The stars go blank in places from the flocks
Of migrating birds too high in the dark to see.

There's melatonin in their pineal glands
Behind their beaks to let them find their way
By sensing minute changes in the light,
Unlike my kind whose senses have become
So insignificant that only words
And widgets thought in words can get us home.

Now cars are made with on-board GPS
So drivers needn't worry with directions,
Reading road signs, having to stop and ask.
And if you watch the sky at night you'll see
The orbits of the satellites that catch
And send the signals of the world, what song
To sing for whom, which urinal to flush.

Back in my truck I hang my head out, looking
More at the constellations than the road
As if to follow my nose and navigate
From star to star, as the crow flies, like geese
And all the hoards of fowl that need no sign
To beat the shortest course from A to Z.

Stevens on the Beach

Southeast, across the Gulf of Mexico
That now belongs to Shell and Texaco,
We know these very waters in Key West
Are those of which he wrote, while at his best,
A poem of enduring elegance
In lines that leave us his intelligence
As if by afterthought or codicil
To some unwritten and unspoken will.

My bride and I have found that while the beach
Impedes our feet like drowsiness on speech
Our thoughts and measured walk go hand in hand.
The mind and body mingle over sand.
We wonder, though, if Stevens also walked
Along this very shore he thought had talked.
Was it this way that he began to think
A female voice had clamored at the brink
Of Florida and incoherent rage?
Did walking barefoot stimulate the sage?

We chuckle at the image. Think of it:
That walrus-like sophistication, fit
For corporate attire, the suit and vest,
Unfettered about the feet and casually dressed.
But still we're certain that the way he strode
Across the beach resembled how he wrote,
His paces taking liberties to vary
While his sense and cadence court and marry.

We're learning that ideas of an order
Often formulate beside a border
That is shifty and impermanent
And yet delineates a continent.
It is a lovely sort of paradox
And we have taken off our shoes and socks
To traipse inside its riddle that combines
A waver and a balance, as in lines
Where Stevens' thought stays limber like a man
Who's walking barefoot in the miles of sand.

Sailing to Horn Island

Today was made of pelicans and light
From *L'Ile Dauphine* to past where *Petit Bois*
Has drifted in the sift and pile of surf.
The day was made like years of yesterdays
Where centuries contend en echelon
By infantries of tide that still inform
The normal course of action here: direct
And westerly collections of the sand
From Appalachian boulders ground to grist
And washed to sea in waterways and floods.
It filters through the silt of Mobile Bay
Until its epaulets are left in layers
Over the migrant islands, wandering west.

We've also followed from the hills and hollows
Of Tennessee to flow by crest and trough
The very path of sand and sediment
That piled these islands into barriers
So long before belonging to the French
That neither man nor beast, nor living language
Can recollect the time they were not there.
But pilgrimage will always take you back
Along a haunted way that time has worn,
And this is a pilgrimage of sand and salt
To find the island of an artist's psalm
That Walter Anderson wrote all in water,
Crazy praise of providence and paint,
If it still lingers there by light or land.

We've seen the sun on gulls and gallinules
And felt the heavy welter of the hull
Beneath our feet. We've known by sheet and knot
That variables of air stayed strong and constant,
All to pitch and yaw by wave and wind
In certain perpendiculars that crossed
As though opposing one another's will
To score the shore with tide from east to west
And heel the keel to keep us in the spray.
But air that carries us and sweeps us west,
And slow hypnosis of our cradle-craft,
Induce a movement also in the mind.
We get a sense that history and story
Join to coin a language made of lilt.
A boat in motion claims its lineage
By riding etymologies of M,
What sailors marked in bark, a first abstraction,
Preceding even Indo-European
When the genesis of words like, "water,"
And "ode" had flowed from one, the cognate *wed*.

Each tack and reach is a literary act,
Returning bow and stern and mast to moorings
In the oldest poems in the canon
Where seafarers wandered out of the way.
Their rhythm was the letter of the law
That deep redundant seas alliterate
As much for us as when the *birth* and *berth*
Of English had embarked from *beran*, to bear.

The noiseless voyage of the day behind,
Together with the set of luff and tiller,

Also writes a kind of line, a language
Spoken only in the motions made
When bodies follow in a tidal flow.
The farther into darkness we sail west
The closer we approach our origin.
The laws of water write in runes that read:
"Our etymology is always light."
We sensed it in the gradients of shade
All afternoon as shadows on the sail
Corrected crescents downward into night
Until the stars were brilliant from our boat.

Now phosphorescent water flickers fire
And sparkles in the darkness where our rudder
Waves the wake and leaves the gulf aglow.
Then we surmise in silence that the lights
So boundlessly surrounding boat and body
Are strewn like stardust sifted out of suns.
Their shine is recognizable in eyes,
The dust of stars in us that Love Divine,
Whose name was nameless and unknowable,
Combined with light and breath to make us bright.

Déjà-vu in Ocean Springs, Mississippi

Home of Walter Anderson, 1903-1965

Was it in August, or not yet; July?
The surf was full of stinging jellyfish,
And tourists left the water for the dunes.
Glare on a parking lot of oyster shells
Had blinded me just momentarily
With head-rush squint and rainbowed dizziness.

I saw the floating speck that's always blind
In everybody's sight, the eye's scotoma
Lining up with a piece of broken glass.
It made a mirror I could see inside,
Revealing something of the place to me
As if it came from someone else's mind:
    An old Impala's hot interior;
    A drive and sidewalk lined with aspidistra,
    Green as flaking paint on shell-back chairs.

It felt like someone else's déjà-vu.
But whose? A ghost of thought? A memory?
Or was it like the genius of the place?
    Shearwater wings cut shadow past the sun.
    Split-second negatives printed paper-like.
Shore bird from '54? Or was it summer,
Eight years later in the Brownie camera
Found with film inside at some yard sale,
Forgotten recollections of a man

Who let the wings take shape in pottery
Then broke the pots? Or did he carve the bird
On slabs of kitchen floor linoleum blocks?
The broken bisque that saw no second glaze;
          The watercolor feathers that were burned . . . .

The artist drew his birds, trying to write
Their living speed instead of paper shapes,
So when he got the gesture from his wrist
He spoke them into life. They're still alive;
I see them while standing here in oyster shells,
Remembering the mother tongue of birds.

Black Skimmers on the Gulf Coast

Rynchops niger

The afternoon increases as it wanes,
And Skimmers, which are named for what they do,
Fly low above the water where they strain
A living morsel they don't need to chew.
Their liquid movements and ecstatic cries
Embody what is lingua franca here,
A place where Name and Motion compromise,
That is, a promise of remaining near.

But sea birds have no use for being named
By *homo sapiens*, ostensibly
In times of greater care for what was framed
When even Man was named more sensibly.
What matters is the movement of the birds.
Their flight is name enough, a substantive
Of verb as noun. Like certain German words,
Their form and function are their genitive.

While Man goes all about acquiring things,
Destroying what he does not understand,
Black Skimmers own the motion of their wings
As it has been for centuries of sand.
The more we own the less we have to name,
Unlike this bird whose flight defines the sea.
While afternoons increase the more they wane,
Black Skimmers skim oblivious of me.

Gulf Coast Reverie

Oysters on the half shell.
Crabs are in the pot.
Tabasco has a sweet smell
And isn't all that hot.

The afternoon was made for beer.
Tonight is made for wine.
Tomorrow is still a blur from here,
And, really, that's just fine.

Walter Anderson on the Chandelleurs

At home, in Ocean Springs, when time itself
Was forced to bide for March, he fed his fires
And rolled his cigarettes all winter long
With watercolors done from memory,
Each one a masterpiece on typing paper.
Draw on the water. Color the sound of joy.

In warmer weather he would brave mosquitoes,
Hurricanes, and oar lock blisters, rowing
Out to sea, due south, then watching west
For Pelicans that lit the Chandelleurs,
The islands where they mated in the gulf.
Hope is an openness that loves your voice.

He stayed for weeks out there, subsisting on
The cans that lost their labels in the boat,
Or what he found at hand. He took what came
By will and wonder, providence in practice,
Living to draw the flying birds he saw.
Draw on the water. Color the sound of joy.

He drew them, yes, but less in an aim to paint
A perfect picture than to catch the breath,
The gesture of a movement with a line,
A single line that perfectly suggested
All of what he didn't need to draw.
Hope is an openness that loves your voice.

He wrote the birds, believing he could name
The moving shapes of each by plain motif,
An archetypal letter that could limn
The creature's aboriginal design,
Its lineage as etymology.
Draw on the water. Color the sound of joy.

So every bird became the first of birds.
Its flesh revealed the essence of itself
Until the painter understood their speech,
The clucks and chuckles of the pelicans
That spelled the eloquence of oyster shells.
Hope is an openness that loves your voice.

Spirit mattered in a living hymn.
Who wouldn't gladly lose his mind to gain
Another, even if it were a bird's,
Especially if the only thing it said were,
Draw on the water. Color the sound of joy.
Hope is an openness that loves your voice.

Dauphin Island in August

For Kathryn

It's easy to imagine here
Between the sea oats and the surf
That water carries more than sound.
We hear a voice that rises clear
And almost human from the swells,
So then to see each wave record
Its fall in analogs of line
Against the surface of the sand,
It seems that what we hear as song
And what we see in tattered foam
Could be a kind of poetry.
It writes a fluid motion down.

The song *I* hear is sensual,
An uncontrollable desire
To be ephemeral and lasting
All at once, incontinent,
Though with a single mate, the sand.
But do *you* hear the song I hear?
If you could read between those lines
Would you know what was on my mind?

It's difficult to walk in sand,
But this velocity of heel
And toe is something we delight
To find each year.
It strikes me now
That it's the very pace you kept

On our wedding day, approaching me
In certain heels, in your handmade dress
Of lace and Shantung silk and veil.
You wanted Bach to make your march,
Concerto number five, the *Largo*,
Played the way Glen Gould had done
In late career, his keen repose
And touch of something passionate,
Though tempered possibly with age.

That's how you came to me, as if
To set the pace that we should tender
One another over time;
And how we're walking now, and how
The waves are falling on the shore.
So what I hear is not the voice
Of someone's falling cadences,
But rhythm turning audible,
The pace of walking in the sand.

I feel no rage to order words
Of water written in the foam.
But if I told you what I hear,
I'd need to draw perspective lines
To find the vanishing point ahead.
What if infinity for pi
Were carried out until the end
The way one scientist supposed
That all the numbers there would make
A pattern-signature of God?
I think we'd see a lighted place,
A room to sit in wicker chairs,

Iced coffee sugared in our glasses,
Then, nearby and audible,
That piece of Bach you've always loved.

IV. The Heart's Arithmetic

At Dauphin Island

It was a year ago, and so much still
Was up in the air, all spiraled out to sea.
And even then I felt things growing still
As, when inside a hurricane, you see
How calm it really is. You notice light
And its delicious undertow.
                                                                    We'd seen
The pine trees full of shine, and shells so slight
That we saw right through them. Such was the scene,
As it had been that day when we began.
It seemed to me at least that something stood
Between us, a lens of light, so I began
To see how close you were. I understood
How circumstance improves a stance, midwife
To sight; how seeing you, I saw my wife.

An Equation for my Children

It may be esoteric and perverse
That I consult Pythagoras to hear
A music tuning in the universe.
My interest in his math of star and sphere
Has triggered theorems too far-fetched to solve.
They don't add up. But if I rack and toil
More in ether than a mortal coil,
It is to comprehend how you revolve
By formulas of orbit, ellipse, and ring.

Dear son and daughter, if I seem to range
It is to chart the numbers spiraling
Between my life and yours until the strange
And seamless beauty of equations click
Solutions for the heart's arithmetic.

Ice Cream Angel

We took our children to the carousel,
A place in town where abandoned factories
Have long-since been replaced with little shops
And restaurants, and now a coffee house.
We rode them round and round until they tired
And clamored for an ice cream cone. "OK,"
I said, "just one, and then we have to go."
Inside the ice cream shop we found our seats
And saw a woman several tables down
Who leaned her chair against the wall and licked
Her cone. At sixty-five, with plastic shoes,
Print dress, a ratty purse, and wiry hair,
She wasn't like the other customers.
She coughed, and something in the sound of it
Had nearly made me vomit. Then she said:
"Y'all's got nice children. Must'a trained 'em right."
I looked around and really shouldn't have;
She had her index finger up her nose
And pulled it out all bloody to the knuckle,
Saying again, "Y'all's got some purdy children."
Then she told us how she'd never married;
"Never had no children;" came from Huntsville
Back in the sixties; worked in factories,
And also "here," this very ice cream shop
That used to be a hardware/mercantile.
She still comes back because she loves the place.
"I gots a ton of memories," she said,
And *didn't* tell us, though I half-way guessed

How she was not so ugly then. I wondered:
Is she an aging prostitute? Did she
Not screw the man who used to own the place
Because he let her live upstairs rent-free?
Was there a time back in the stockroom dark
When he had hiked her dress, when she had thought
For just a second that she loved the man?
My dirty mind imagined how she did,
Why she comes back, for love, the way she felt
Alive inside the body he desired.
I had her number.
                    But just before we left,
We heard, "Y'all must be doing something right.
Yer kids are gonna be just fine...don't worry."
The hair rose up on the back of my neck. We *had*
Been worried, hadn't we? The children. The ache
Of them, carved as they were like pretty horses
That circled us and waited for the chance
To gallop off.
                    Did someone say, "Fear not?"
Not quite, but almost that. I whipped around,
But she was gone as if she'd disappeared.
And isn't that what angels do, the extra-
Ordinary in the ordinary,
The supernatural made natural?
I won't forget her cough and bloody finger,
The glisten on her snaggle tooth,
Eyes closed, the smile gone bodiless
To spoon our palms, our necks,
The arches of our feet.

Jack Daniel in the Lions' Den

Behind us in the car, my son who's three
Has mashed a story of the Holy Ghost
Together with the spirit of Tennessee.
We laugh then realize that, more than most,
Our boy has understood the story's gist.
He says, "Jack Daniel in the lions' den,"
As if the kernel of truth in words is grist
For him to grind between his teeth, so when
He's made them into meal that's fit for bread,
Or even drink as in our local whiskey,
Their meanings blend together in his head
So well they aren't presumptuous or risky.

The Holy Spirit is a kind of drink.
It does intoxicate believers' hearts
And even lions, as when over the brink
In Babylon, it guarded Daniel's parts.
And it's distilled in children's tongues like food,
In words with texture that is chewable
Such that the sound combines with how it's chewed
To reach a meaning that is spiritual.
So if we taste a phrase as children do,
Both epic narrative and anecdote
Inebriate and feed by ringing true.
When sound makes sense, it's the perfect antidote
To roaring lies.
Then on to something else,
My son asks, "Daddy, what's beyond the sky?"

And I can't tell him anything that tells
The answer it would take and will not try.

The Genius of Hardin County

For J.H.

Often in the evening close to dusk,
He tracks a deer where no one saw a deer
In someone's field that is no more a field.
Deep in the Hardin County woods, he's seen
A stream that leaps and doesn't ever land.
The earth below it opens like a throat,
Swallowing the downpour rush of water,
Silently cutting through the fossil record.

He's on a mission, trying to find a word
That names exactly what the water does,
What inexplicably resurfaces
Again as vapor in the battlefields.
He follows where it takes a shape again,
Of breath in front of deer, or washes back
In gaping formlessness behind a crow.
He tracks the word along the memories
Of older men beside their fathers' barns.
He lifts a cistern brick up close to his ear
To hear the echoes hiding in the clay,
The bell sound grown-ups never know exists
And children never lose.
                                        Below his feet,
The arrowheads and *minié* balls have been
Plowed up so many times they almost share
A common thread that only *seems* coherent

After it rains, their shiny points in sod
Like moonshine burning in a horse's eye.
He looks in there and sees the murder scene
At Pickwick Lake; they dredged around the dock
And found a mailbox, then another, then
Another, several hundred in the end.
Each one belonged to someone who was dead,
The names and numbers legible, and some
Had rotten letters still inside, the flags
Still up with undelivered mail.
He sees
The pregnant woman's naked body tangled
In weeds and trot lines where the flood had risen;
Sees the coiled-up papery remains
Of rattlesnakes around a breaker box,
Reminding him that safety is a lie,
That is, until he's touched the nerve, and found
The perfect word to name the peril: "Danger."
Its history can tame a fear with joy.
Watch when a sparrow flies across the sun,
Wings lit, both held and melted there at once,
Printing the letter of its brief eclipse
Mid-air, before it passes back to bird.
Just say the word that tells you what it is
And feel the holy fire that burns
Behind the animal it spelled.
Pronounce it like my friend
Who calls it "Joy."

My Queen of Hearts

The other day our daughter lay on the ground
And watched the clouds that shuffled over her.

Sky was the glassy palace where she crowned
Her golden hair with twisted hay and clover.

She looked like girlhood photographs of you,
But since I never knew you as a child,
I wondered if the picture in my head was true:
    You as a princess with your aces wild,
    Not yet the noble woman next to me.

Throughout the years now woven in between,
I've played the joker, feigning regency,
But here, full house, with you as queen,
Your heart from girlhood lives in our young lass
Who gave you the crown she made of braided grass.

Monorhyme for my Wife at Forty

"O, love's best habit is in seeming trust,
And age in love loves not to have years told."
— Shakespeare, sonnet 138

She tells me how she *needs* her beauty sleep,
A lie, but I've seen her sleeping late and deep
When everyone is up and has to creep
In sock feet all around the house to keep
From waking her.
But what is "beauty sleep?"
Was being young expendable and cheap
To make the price of middle age so steep?

She swears, "No, really, I just *need* my sleep,"
So I believe her if she lies to keep
The cost of aging down. Do I not reap
The benefit by sight, as when I sweep
Her covers back and feel my innards leap?

Though beauty *needs* no rest to stay this deep,
I lie along with her and let her sleep.

Buying Your Perfume

"The silver apples of the moon,
The golden apples of the sun."
— W.B. Yeats

It can't be something obvious to most —
More subtle like the revenant or ghost
Of a flower, lingering after the air and dew
Of dawns that are no more.
The wine of yearning . . .
The memory of apples . . .

And so with this I'll look for you
In all the little gardens of the morning.

The Flower Beds of War

Fort Gaines, Dauphin Island, Alabama

Today, as in that war we christened "civil,"
Spring arrives around these magazines.
Examine the cannon mounts that used to swivel;
The tidal flushing of its brick latrines;

And look where violets and grass have spread
Beside the ramparts facing west and east.
Was it not so when soldiers there fell dead,
When only flax and thistles kept the peace?

Can we distinguish flower from the weed
When each is uniformed in blue or dun,
On battlefields, or in the human seed,
Where life and death are waging to be won?

We rage and kill and also love and bless.
One grows around the other, truce and bruise,
And can't be separated, not unless
We silence one and lose them both, and lose

This relic of antique belligerence
That nature calls a garden, we a fort,
Where spring, in its sublime indifference,
Has flanked the guns with clumps of spiderwort.

Love Time, My Daughter!

From a line of anonymous German poetry

Hüte dich, schönes Blümelein!
Protect yourself, my pretty little flower;
Time is the wound *and* healer, by design,

By secrets we can't decipher or divine.
It loves you to death with its destructive power.
Hüte dich, schönes Blümelein!

That garden path we planted in a line
Of brick to your imaginary bower,
It wounded time through heal-all, columbine,

Muguet, and wild Virginia creeper vine;
It leads to a timely *and* untimely hour.
Hüte dich, schönes Blümelein!

We can't untangle how the stars align,
But we can love them back when the heavens glower
Down on us. Love heals the wounded sign

That's written on your water, makes you wine.
Delight in the weed *and* garden, what years devour!
Hüte dich, schönes Blümelein!
Time heals all wounds it makes, dear bloom of mine.

Benjamin Shooting Skeet

Eleven years have led to this.
You break the gun, eject a shell,
Reload, and stand there saying, "Pull!"

"Joy" is being caught in the act
Of never asking what it means.
It's just a game to you, a trick
Of sending one more pigeon out
To pulverize.
                                    The thrill is seeing
Your skill rewarded instantly.

The art of it is how to swing
Your barrel *past* the target, then
To shoot the empty space in front,
The place the moving skeet will be.
It matters how you try to miss.

My joy is that I almost forget
How target clays were *made* to break;
That effort isn't always paid;
That you will learn, as I once did,
How it's not a game at all.
                                                                    It's war,
The constant *aristeia* mode
Of being male, the history
Of arrow, spear, atlatl, bolt,
And bullet hiding in your eye.

The game of life is "life and death"
And played across the simple ways
A man can hit or miss the mark:
Outlandish women and booze, both
On the rocks, singing in your veins
For you to be the schooner captain
Snookered to dock with them for good.

The pleasures of this world are hints
Of deeper feelings in the next.

Beware of strawman arguments,
Cheap praise, sure bets, and easy gain.

The line between success and failure,
Son, is Timing more than Line.

Remember that even falling short
Reminds you where the target is.

Take aim and fire. Delight in that.
Each gaffe you make can turn to good.

Remember how it feels to be,
And not yet know that you've become,

An artist of *hamartia*
And heart.

From Lookout Mountain at Night

I.
Before the slow descent to Ruby Falls,
We stop and watch the sprawl of city lights.
I think of lines on someone's palm enlarged
Like a traffic map, each intersection lit
In different colors.
                    My son, who's four years old,
Says, "Christmas lights," his way to register
How a powered urban grid both tarnishes
The shine of evening stars and copies it
As artificial novas on the ground.
But tonight, the view comes slowly into focus
As mercury vapors, white hot halogens,
And headlight-taillight bulbs that overlap
With obstacles of trees and power poles,
Foreshortened and enlarged in ever-changing
Vantage points we make as we descend.

That's how it *is* but, still, I can't respond
Except by saying what I think it's *like,*
Like stars, or Christmas lights in someone's palm.
Is metaphor a memory, two things
Remembering when they were both the same?
Consider the stars, no, all things far apart;
By a common trait or someone's turn of phrase,
They leap together in the linker's mind,

A backwards bang that reunites the light
That shines as various and sundry suns,

II.
Not far from here, some twenty years ago,
A teacher showed me where, in the Civil War,
Beleaguered Union troops had bivouacked.
They dug a shallow plot for every tent,
Staying no more than several days before
They moved again.
                    Year upon year of leaves
Dissolved, filling the beds with nothing but time.
In 1988, I knelt beside them
And let my fingers trace the places where
Each soldier slept before he lived or died.
I'd like to show it to my son and share
The same collective memory if it
Has not been turned into a parking lot.

What does it mean if we remember things
We've covered up, demolished, or erased?
If, once the "thing" is gone, will memory
Be cancelled out, a double negative?
And where are memories that we forget?
Are they recorded in inverted Braille?
Or in the language of the major apes,
The one they can't invent, so can't pronounce
The fact that This is not at all like That?
Or in the forest here where fossil ferns
Still lie entangled in the roots' intrigue,
Fossils that look so much like living ferns,

Remembering the soil in the stone,
That even the humid air we breathe tonight
Remembers by its own analogy
That Chattanooga was once an ancient sea
That's now the salty water in our lungs?

III.
So once we see that lines across a palm
Are like the remaining veins in fossil leaves
And like the pattern of a city's streets,
We find the place where Memory and Time
Are just a double-sided metaphor.

A memory is like a lack of time,
And time is like a dream I can't recall,
And Metaphor is how the three are joined,
And all of them are where my son will be
When I am gone, when he looks in his hands
And sees imaginary maps of land,
Of everything he's held and couldn't hold,
Of worlds he'll find ethereal and real
All locked in orbits by the gravity
That makes his bones remember the gist of me,
What he'll become, a living simile
Of what I was in essence and in pith,
A soldier sleeping in the Christmas lights.

Anniverse 13

For Kathryn

Between the wedding, or the wedding night,
And the sixtieth, diamond anniversary,
There are the lesser days we often slight:
The sixth of iron, the ninth of pottery,
The tenth of tin, the fifth of wood or clocks.
Only the blessed at thirty-five or more
Achieve the marriages of precious rocks:
Jade, ruby, sapphire, or the golden ore.
Tonight we celebrate our special day,
And celebrate how it has taken grace,
Not luck; we've lasted thirteen years today,
Our thirteenth anniversary of Lace.

It's serendipitous, no less; this "prime,"
The most unlucky number, makes us think
Of something that's both subtle and sublime.
At least when lifted up, who wouldn't wink,
Or nod to modesty and moral laws,
And gaze at what should chance to lie behind
(Or not) a looped and knotted lens of gauze:
A table top, a bed, or you reclined.
It's even fortunate that something less-
Than-sheer should come between my eyes and you.
Just as your wedding veil and lacy dress
Obscured your body, it also brought in view
The kind of vision some men have when they
First see the woman they were meant to wed.
It's both projection from the wedding day

To all the life they'll share until they're dead,
And also panning backwards, as with me,
I caught a glimpse of your progenitors
And saw the woman who was certainly
The first to carry traits that now are yours.
A thousand years ago, she turned the heads
Of men who saw her and forgot their lovers.
At home, she made the bed with lovely spreads,
Then loved her man to sleep and stole the covers.

Time is a filmy curtain always drawn
Between what has and hasn't yet expired,
Obscuring view from viewer, and turning us on
By how it leaves a lot to be desired.
With every year, we leave the lucky lace
And earn the rocks and minerals of life,
But, if by grace or luck, each time I see your face
The veil is lifted, my once and future wife.

Thanksgiving on the Gulf

After the hurricane we took our walks
And found that every other house was gone
From waves that only left the crooked stalks
Of pilings where the beach was built upon.

And as we walked along the shifting line
Between the wreckage and the surf and spray,
It struck me that so much of what is mine
Is built on sand or less-than-solid clay.

I've staked a claim, set up a corner post,
And checked the plumb, then seen it teeter free
Of vertical, like me, too near the coast
Between my balance and catastrophe.

And even the steps we took along the beach
Erected columns, hopelessly forestalling,
Sight unseen, what gravity would teach:
That merely walking is an act of falling,

Then of falling back in balance, foot
To foot, a pattern *and* a latitude.
Since I'm resigned to never staying put,
Surrender is the purest gratitude.

Audare/Audire

Nine-tenths of wisdom lies in listening;
It almost matters more than what you see.
The other tenth is knowing when to sing
The truth, the timing of pure audacity.

Recordari-Song

The summer house was being sold,
And I told my daughter, "Remember this!"
She looked and smiled; at three years old,
She didn't know what she could miss.

I tried to plant the treasure clue
That she could find another day.
"Remember this," I said, "so you
Will have it when you're old! Okay?"

Her eyes were full of sky, but what
Could they have held? If I had died,
Could all her doors to *me* have shut
In time no matter how she tried?

Did thinking that make me a ghost
Or retroactively erased?
Or was I something at her coast
Of Thens and Nows that would be traced?

Two years, and Hurricane Katrina
Shredded the house she couldn't forget
And dumped its wood in the marina
As if to unrecord Regret

And Thing at once, all memory drowned.
But a "record" calls to *cor*, to heart
And makes a song of what it found.
Let past and present come apart!

My daughter has learned a way to plant them,
Her treasure troves of time and space.
Like a troubadour, she'll find them and chant them,
Singing the pieces back in place.

The Author

WIL MILLS, the son of agricultural missionaries, grew up in Brazil and Louisiana. After earning his BA and MA in theology from the University of the South, he worked at a variety of jobs, including carpenter, sawmill operator, and baker. He also served as the Kenan Visiting Writer at the University of North Carolina at Chapel Hill, and as the Writer-in-Residence at Covenant College in Chattanooga. His poetry was published in *Poetry*, *The New Republic*, *The Hudson Review*, *The New Criterion*, and many other journals. His debut collection, *Light for the Orphans*, was published in 2002, and his *Selected Poems* in 2013. Until his death in 2011, he lived in Tennessee with his wife Kathryn and their two children, Benjamin and Phoebe-Agnès, first in a house that he built himself in Sewanee, then, later, in Chattanooga.

www.ingramcontent.com/pod-product-compliance
Lightning Source LLC
Chambersburg PA
CBHW030427310726
48979CB00009B/1659/J